Secrets

SACRED SECRETS
A Living Proof Live Experience

BETH MOORE

LifeWay Press®
Nashville, Tennessee

Published by LifeWay Press®

© 2013 • Beth Moore

ISBN 978-1-4300-3093-5

Item 005627186

Dewey decimal classification: 248.843

Subject headings: SECRECY \ CHRISTIAN LIFE \ WOMEN

Unless indicated otherwise, all Scripture quotations are taken from the Holy Bible, English Standard Version, copyright © 2000, 2001 by Crossway Bibles, a division of Good News Publishers. Scripture marked HCSB Copyright © 1999, 2000, 2002, 2003, 2009 by Holman Bible Publishers. Used by permission. Holman Christian Standard Bible® and HCSB® are federally registered trademarks of Holman Bible Publishers. Scripture marked NKJV is from the New King James Bible—New Testament. Copyright © 1979, 1982, Thomas Nelson, Inc., Publishers.

To order additional copies of this resource, write to LifeWay Church Resources, Customer Service, One LifeWay Plaza, Nashville, TN 37234-0113; fax 615.251.5933; phone 800.458.2772; order online at *www.lifeway.com* or email *orderentry@lifeway.com;* or visit the LifeWay Christian Store serving you.

Printed in the United States of America

Adult Ministry Publishing

LifeWay Church Resources

One LifeWay Plaza

Nashville, TN 37234-0152

DEDICATION

To Paige Greene, my beloved friend and fellow sojourner, for believing God feverishly with me for this message. Jesus Christ alone could have fed the zeal we all still feel toward this long-lived partnership in serving women. I am crazy about you, Paige. May God keep our knees down, our faces up, and our hands reaching out.

ABOUT THE AUTHOR

Beth Moore is an author and Bible teacher of best-selling Bible studies and books for women. She is the founder of Living Proof Ministries and speaker at Living Proof Live women's events across the U.S. Beth's mission is to guide women everywhere into a richer, more fulfilling relationship with the Father.

CONTENTS

INTRODUCTION

When we shared the Living Proof Life event in Greensboro, I think we all grew wide-eyed with the sense that God was doing something important in our lives. After the experience, we jointly came to the conclusion that He desired to do a work broader than the walls of that arena. After significant confirmation from the Lord, the LifeWay team and I began working together to take this weekend teaching and create a space in it for you. You were in our hearts every step of the way, and we pray with everything in us that God will reveal Himself through the experience.

I believe God wants to do something deeper in a holy secrecy than can be contained in a weekend. We need time to study His Word and to digest the topic of sacred secrets. To do that, we first broke the event video into five sessions with some bonus segments so it can be used in a group. Then I've taken portions of the material in the weekend and sought to unpack them through several written elements.

The first thing you'll see through this volume is that it has the character of a journal. I do dearly love a new journal. Don't you? We've left you lots of room to talk with God through writing out your thoughts and what you sense the Holy Spirit teaching you. Then rather than a more traditional study, I've tried to give you short catalysts for thought, prayer, and action.

You'll find word studies on some of the terms in Scripture that revolve around the topic. You'll also find questions and a number of verses to stimulate your own study.

Will you humor me as I say that, through the video portion of this series, you will also find a wardrobe malfunction? I'm supposed to watch my video portions before I sign off on them to be published, but I can never make it through more than five minutes. I hate watching myself. When I viewed a few seconds of the opening session, my jaw dropped because my white jeans looked like leggings and my top looked like a short skirt. It somehow did not look that way in the hotel mirror. In case you stumble easily over wrong wardrobe choices, let me say before you ever push play on the video: No, those are not leggings. They're jeans. But I'm not wearing them again on tape. Laughing. But only a little.

My prayer is that you will go beyond what can be accomplished at an event and walk forward into a relationship with Christ that is exceedingly more intimate and rewarding. May God invite you to embrace a whole new journey with Him in the secret places where He longs for you to find Him.

Beth

WEEK 1

THE THEOLOGY
OF SECRECY

I hope you'll find great joy in these pages. We'll revisit some of the ideas we talked about in the video sessions, slowing down so you can take them apart and apply them. I'll be asking you some questions or adding some ideas for you to contemplate. And we'll dip into the rich well of the biblical terms God uses for *secret*.

Neither the Old Testament nor the New Testament has a word that corresponds perfectly to the English word *secret*. Rather, we will see that the Bible uses a large number of descriptive terms that may be translated with one of the forms of the word *secret*. You'll find multiple translations very helpful in this regard. I highly recommend using a parallel Bible. One may translate a given word as *secret* while others use *hiding place, shelter, friend,* or *even treasure.* Please don't be put off or intimidated by this process. Once you get into the original meanings, I think you'll love the dimensions they bring to the concept. A great wealth will unfold before you as you delve into the biblical terms.

You'll note I've left you a great deal of room for your own thoughts. If you watch the video segments, you'll have heard plenty from my big mouth, but what is most vital is that you hear straight from God without any human interference. You'll do that best as you contemplate His Word and spend time with Him one-on-one. Make these pages your own. If my thoughts help, then praise God. If something doesn't connect, then go on to the next thing. This isn't intended to be as progressive as a normal study. I just want to supply you some truths to stimulate your time with the One who is Truth.

I wish I could be there with you face-to-face, but in some ways, as you'll soon discover, that would defeat the purpose. Instead we'll each walk into this journey seeking a glorious encounter with Jesus, the Lover of our souls and the Knower of our hearts.

THE THEOLOGY OF SECRECY

SECRET: What kind of _____ does that word
have in you?

Every _____ word is good news.

The Theology of Secrecy: _____ _____

Our triumphs and our defeats erupt from our
_____.

Key verse: Psalm 51:6

"Behold, you delight in truth in the inward
being, and you teach me wisdom
in the secret heart" (Ps. 51:6).

Our prayer: Lord, You teach me wisdom in the secret.

Do you love the _____?

Secrets in Old Testament:	Secrets in the Gospels	Secrets from Acts to Revelation:
Mostly _____	Mostly _____	Mostly _____

Point 1: There are _____ secrets and there are _____ secrets.

Video sessions available for purchase at
www.lifeway.com/sacredsecrets

Hebrew Word Study

The most commonly used Hebrew term for *secret* in the Old Testament is *çether* (סֵתֶר). The meanings of the word can include: "a cover" (in a good or a bad, a literal or a figurative sense), "covering," "hiding place," "shelter," "protection," or "secret place."

A secret can be a wonderful or a terrible thing, and it can be an utterly beautiful thing. The following two verses illustrate the difference perfectly.

> "The person who makes a carved idol or cast image, which is detestable to the LORD, the work of a craftsman, and sets it up in secret (*çether*, סֵתֶר) is cursed" (Deut. 27:15).

> "You are my hiding place (*çether*, סֵתֶר);
> You protect me from trouble.
> You surround me with joyful shouts
>   of deliverance" (Ps. 32:7).

How would you explain that a secret, on the one hand, could be detestable to the Lord and, on the other hand, something He Himself could virtually embody?

Are you just a little bit relieved that God doesn't just destroy the concept of secrecy and leave us totally exposed? If yes, how so?

If you've heard the suggestion that everything you've ever done or thought would ultimately be shown to everyone, does God's endorsement of some kinds of secrecy encourage you just a bit? Explain.

Our basic thesis is that **secrets manifest.** Say those last two words several times out loud so they'll begin to go in your thoughts from pencil to permanent marker. We will see that the one way we can be absolutely certain something will show up outwardly is to take it into the secret part of our lives.

For starters, think about that principle in the human realm. In what ways do the things we so want to keep secret end up manifesting themselves anyway in one or more of the following areas of our lives? Let's really give these some thought:

How do secrets show up through physical results in our bodies?

How do secrets show up through our personal relationships?

How do secrets show up in our parenting?

How do secrets show up in our ability to trust people?

How do secrets show up in our ability to trust God?

Did you notice that one of the meanings of *çether* is shelter? How can a secret be either a shelter of protection or a shelter of darkness plaguing our lives and hiding us from the light?

Look at some of the other Old Testament passages using *çether* (סֵתֶר).

> "He who dwells in the shelter
> (*çether*, סֵתֶר) of the Most High
> will abide in the shadow of
> the Almighty" (Ps. 91:1).

How has the Most High been a protection or shelter to you recently?

Have there been ways you feel that God has not been a protection to you? He knows He's been there all along in your priceless life, but He wants you to come to a greater assurance of it, too. He wants you to pour your heart out to Him if you're struggling to believe.

If you need to ask where He was at a certain time or season, Beloved Sister, go ahead and do it! It will do your soul good and, in the days and months to come, watch for Him to give you glimpses and glances of His closeness to you at those times of your life.

Recently I found a letter my grandmother wrote to me at a very painful season in my childhood when she had no idea what I had endured. I felt it was a gift of God illustrating how He'd placed people in my life to show such love to me. Watch for Him to do those kinds of things as you open your eyes to His tenderness toward you.

Oh, Sister, God loves you so much. Even the fact that you're in His Word right this very moment is proof that He will never let you go.

If it's true that what's vaulted in us is the seat of our triumphs and our defeats, then consider the following:

What may be vaulted in you that causes you great stress or shame?

What may be vaulted in you that you need to embrace and appreciate?

What may be vaulted in you that you need to get to know?

If we need tending, how might tending our vaults be a little bit …

1. like cleaning out old clutter?

2. like draining an abscess?

3. like gathering treasures we'd long lost?

> "I will give you the treasures of darkness
>   and the hoards in secret places,
>   that you may know that it is I, the LORD,
>   the God of Israel, who call you
>   by your name" (Isa. 45:3).

"My frame was not hidden from you,
when I was being made in secret,
intricately woven in the depths
of the earth" (Ps. 139:15).

In what sense do you get great comfort from the realization that God knows you completely?

In what sense does God's complete knowledge of you cause you discomfort? (Me, too, so let's just squirm together while we describe how we feel.)

Hebrew Word Study

Another Hebrew term sometimes translated *secret* is the word *çowd* (סוֹד), meaning a session, i.e. company of persons (in close deliberation); by implication, intimacy, consultation, a secret assembly or secret counsel.

Psalm 25:14 says,

> "The secret counsel of the LORD
>   is for those who fear Him,
> and He reveals His covenant
>   to them" (HCSB).

Compare the words of Psalm 25:14 with Isaiah 48:16:

> "I have not spoken in secret."

In what ways is the truth of God open knowledge?

In what ways is the truth of God closed to outsiders?

Following the Parable of the Sower (see Matt. 13:3-9), the disciples asked why Jesus taught in parables. He told them:

> "To you it has been given to know the secrets
>   of the kingdom of heaven, but to them
>   it has not been given" (Matt. 13:11).

What do you think would be the basis for Christ revealing "secrets of the kingdom of heaven" to some and not to others?

What does it mean to you to be an insider with Jesus, that He wants you to be part of His inner circle?

In the New Testament we find the statement that Mary "treasured up all these things (concerning Jesus) in her heart" (Luke 2:51).

Why might it be important and valuable to keep and treasure some secrets?

Why is keeping appropriate confidences so important?

How would you explain to a younger woman or your daughter how she could tell the difference between keeping confidence and protecting a lie? (Plan to discuss this with your group.)

Let's reflect back on the statement "every gospel word is a good word" and how it would be biblically possible to make such a claim. The word *gospel* means "good news" so, because of Jesus Christ who brought it and fleshed it out, every single word it speaks over any situation or condition is ultimately good.

Read Colossians 1:3-6 and jot down ways the segment could prove the point:

Have you ever had to deal with someone with whom you never knew where you stood? Yep, me too. If so, how did that affect the relationship?

How do God's definitive statements contrast to dealing with the uncertainty of people?

You never need to walk on eggshells with God.

Hebrew Word Study

The Psalmists often repeated related concepts with slightly different words. In Psalm 27, note another word revolving around the concept of *secrecy*. The Hebrew word *tsaphan* (צָפַן) means "to hide" or "treasure up" ("conceal," "concealed," "hid," "hidden," "hide," or "keep secretly").

> "For He will conceal [there's that
> word *tsaphan*] me in His shelter
> in the day of adversity;
> He will hide me under the cover
> (*cathar*, סָתַר) of His tent;
> He will set me high on a rock" (Ps. 27:5).

From what do you need God to hide or conceal you today?

How does using the first meaning of the word *tsaphan* change the way Psalm 27:5 speaks to you: "He will *treasure me up* in His shelter in the day of adversity"?

What do you think it would take to really have the fact that God treasures you filter all the way through your being?

Proverbs 25:2 says:

> "It is the glory of God to conceal things,
> but the glory of kings is to
> search things out" (HCSB).

The above verse came up in my prayer time this very morning, and I nearly burst at the seams thinking about it in the context of the journey you and I are taking together. I hope to prove to you that God created our minds with a curious bent so we would crave a search. We're literally wired by God to wonder.

You've just got to read Acts 17:26-27. Where were our searching minds meant by God to take us?

A friend tells of playing "treasure hunt" with her grandchildren. When she knows they are coming over she composes a set of rhyming clues, each leading to the next. The game turns out to be as great a joy to the adult as the children. Similarly, God knows the joy that only comes when together you seek to find the treasures He has planned for you. He is not playing a malicious game of hide and seek with the things you need.

Write about a time when greater joy came because you had to seek what God had for you.

"For the idolaters eagerly seek all these things, and your heavenly Father knows that you need them. But seek first the kingdom of God and His righteousness, and all these things will be provided for you" (Matt. 6:32-33, HCSB).

Will you pray the prayer of Psalm 51:6? Father, I know "you delight in truth in the inward being." Will You please "teach me wisdom in the secret"?

SISTER,

I've got to tell you what happened today because I think God appointed it. The timing was too perfect to be a coincidence. I was at home getting ready for work and the Lord brought something to my mind about our concept that I wanted to make sure I remembered. I grabbed a pen and jotted a note to myself and, instead of writing "Sacred Secrets," I'd reversed the letters and written "Scared Secrets."

I stared at it slack-jawed. That very moment I knew God had caused me to stumble on the entire purpose of our journey. This process is going to be all about switching those letters. God is going to take us from a place of being SCARED of our secrets to the glorious light of SACRED secrets. How can we not love a God like that?

WEEK 2

AUTHENTIC INTIMACY

In my study of secrecy in Scripture, I've been so wonderfully surprised to find the positive side of the concept. God intends secrets. He treasures the secret place. He wants to hear your secrets, and He wants to share His secrets with you.

God values the whole secret concept because He values intimacy. His entire work of creation and redemption is for the purpose of genuine intimacy. And that wonderful divine intimacy is so much more than the sleazy exposure our culture has come to confuse with genuine relationship.

Intimacy can't be rushed. It takes time to grow. Isn't it somehow not only refreshing but relieving to know that the God who created you wants to take the time for your relationship to grow?

Thank you for allowing me to share with you through our video time together. Let's spend this week letting Jesus clarify the difference between bad and good secrets. Let's take the time for Him to use His Word to heal our bad secrets and to reveal His good ones.

I'm so glad you're my Sister on this journey. Pull up a chair. Grab your Bible, and let's get started.

AUTHENTIC INTIMACY

Recap:
The Theology of Secrecy: Secrets Manifest

Point 1: There are bad secrets and there are good secrets.

Point 2: A bad secret can be the _____ of us.

Our _____ has no greater success than in our secrets.

Authenticity with _____

Transparency with _____

Intimacy with _____

Our _____ life has to match our _____ life.

Point 3: No secret has to stay _____.

Three terms used for *sin* in Psalm 32:

Sin, _____, and Transgression

Three terms used for *forgiveness* in Psalm 32:

Forgiven, Covered, and _____

Homework:

Let's find a place where we can be all alone and free to voice our confessions of sin to our gracious and merciful Father. Remember, He already knows and He's never let us go. For us to verbalize where we know we've sinned is our means of thinking each transgression through and acknowledging that we have wandered from the will of God and want to turn our course back to Him in each way.

Our genuine confessions and true repentance are means of bringing our sins right to the altar of sacrifice where provision has been made for us. Here we cry out and acknowledge that we want every barrier to divine fellowship and joy removed. Listen, Sister, this is what the cross of Christ was for. Let's not be too proud or too ashamed to say how much we require what He's already accomplished for us. Christ's death on the cross was enough no matter how far we've wandered or how deep a pit we've dug for ourselves. If it were not, I'd be a lost cause, and the last place you'd find me is here in Bible study with you.

Video sessions available for purchase at
www.lifeway.com/sacredsecrets

Point 1: There are bad secrets and there are good secrets.

Point 2: A bad secret can be the death of us.

Another Hebrew word related to our concept of *secret* or *secrecy* appears in Job 4:12 where Eliphaz, Job's questionable friend, was trying to convince him that Job's misfortune was punishment for sin. Eliphaz said:

> "A word was brought to me in secret; my ears caught a whisper of it" (Job 4:12, HCSB).

Hebrew Word Study

The phrase translated "brought to me in secret" is from the word *ganab* (גָּנַב), meaning "to thieve (literally or figuratively)," "to deceive," "to secretly bring," "to steal away," or "to get by stealth."

In what sense can our secrets steal away our lives?

Psalm 10 uses another prominent Hebrew word for *secrecy*. It says of the wicked:

> "He sits in ambush in the villages;
>   in hiding places he murders the innocent.
> His eyes stealthily watch for the
>   helpless" (Ps. 10:8).

Hebrew Word Study

The word for *secret place* is *miçtar* (מִסְתָּר). It means "a concealer" or "a hiding place, particularly one used of the place of ambush."

Our Enemy has no greater success than in our secrets. He builds fortresses for himself in our secret places. When Satan works in the open he has to wear a disguise, but when he works in the dark he can be himself.

How have you experienced him building a fortress in your secret places?

Jeremiah 23 speaks of our attempts to hide ourselves in the secret hiding place:

> "Am I a God at hand, declares the LORD, and
> not a God far away? Can a man hide himself
> in secret places so that I cannot see him?
> declares the LORD. Do I not fill heaven and
> earth? declares the LORD" (Jer. 23:23-24).

Why is the impossibility of hiding from God both a terrible and a comforting truth?

"If your brother, the son of your mother, or your son or your daughter or the wife you embrace or your friend who is as your own soul entices you secretly . . ." (Deut. 13:6).

Why do you think those who are closest to us have the most power to lead us astray?

How have you found the one with whom you're most intimate can entice you more than others?

What have you learned that can help you to mentor a younger believer to avoid false intimacy on the one hand and dangerous isolation on the other?

We have got to be careful about instant intimacy.

Why do you think God's way is revelation rather than exhibition? What benefits come from taking it slow?

THE LADDER OF INTIMACY

A friend once said healthy relationships involve what she called "the ladder of intimacy." Picture two people carrying the relationship up the sides of the ladder. If one gets ahead of the other, the relationship spills.

We can only climb the ladder to the degree that our friend climbs also. Some relationships are only first- or second-step friendships. Each relationship must be treated uniquely, only going as far as each person progresses over time.

On the Ladder of Intimacy, what happens if you desire to go to step 5 with someone who only wants to go to step 2?

What happens if the other person is only trustworthy to ascend to step 3?

What happens if you or the other person rushes the intimacy, trying to run up the ladder?

If the other person doesn't desire to ascend as far up the ladder of intimacy as you do, does that mean you can't be friends? Express your thoughts.

We're not called to intimacy with our entire social network.

> "The wise of heart will receive
> commandments, but a babbling fool
> will come to ruin" (Prov. 10:8).

> "A fool's displeasure is known
> at once . . ." (Prov. 12:16, HCSB).

> "Therefore, the wise person
> will keep silent at such a time, for the
> days are evil" (Amos 5:13, HCSB).

> "Set a guard, O LORD, over my mouth;
> keep watch over the door of
> my lips!" (Ps. 141:3).

AUTHENTICITY WITH ALL
TRANSPARENCY WITH MOST
INTIMACY WITH SOME

Our exterior life has to match our interior life.

Why does the space of contradictions between
our interior life and our exterior life give extreme
opportunity to the Devil?

We don't have to tell it all, but we have to live in such a way that is
honest before people and not contradictory.

Point 3: No secret has to stay bad.

Write your thoughts about the three terms used for *sin* and the three terms for *forgiveness,* or cleansing of sin, in Psalm 32:

Transgression

Sin

Iniquity

Forgiven

Covered

Not Counted

"Take words of repentance with you
and return to the LORD.
Say to Him: 'Forgive all our sin
and accept what is good,
so that we may repay You
with praise from our lips'" (Hos. 14:2, HCSB).

Why do you suppose Hosea 14:2 specifies that in repenting before God we are to "take words" with us?

"So teach us to number our days that we may get a heart of wisdom" (Ps. 90:12).

We touched on this earlier, but with these rich terms from Psalm 32 now in discussion and the interesting wording of Hosea 14:2, let's revisit the concept. If we haven't recently gotten alone with God to unload the weight of our sins, let's do it now. Find a private space and acknowledge every transgression burdening you or blocking your sense of divine fellowship. You don't have to write them, though you might wish to do so, even in code only for yourself.

Sometimes I spill my confessions all out on paper before Him through my words and then shred the page as I imagine the power of the cross shredding every record of my sins. Think about doing something similar if it would help. I need all the help I can get.

Maybe you feel the same way. As you confess verbally, you may want to write about the treasures you wish to bring from the darkness.

WEEK 3

THE REWARDS OF
THE SECRET PLACE

Are you having even a shred of the fun I am with this subject? I'm relieved, intrigued, and exhilarated at the same time.

In this segment of our time together let's get started exploring the rewards of the secret place with Jesus. This is about to be a blast. What an incredible God we serve. Over and over He demonstrates that He can turn our fears and our shame inside out and make of them something we value more than life itself.

If, like me, you come out of this time of Bible study with a joy over the treasures God brings from our darkness instead of a fear of that darkness, we will have had a great journey. Let's be brave enough to look a bit at our own hearts, but let's be wise enough to focus our eyes on the one Who waits for us in secret.

Isn't it incredibly like our God that we can walk with Him for decades and He can still delight us with surprises we haven't yet encountered? This is a new, fresh journey for me. I hope it resonates with you in a similar way.

Let's go see what rewards Christ Jesus has in store for us.

THE REWARDS OF THE SECRET PLACE

Recap:
The Theology of Secrecy: Secrets Manifest

Our prayer: Lord, You teach me wisdom in the secret.

Point 1: There are bad secrets and there are good secrets.

Point 2: A bad secret can be the death of us.

Point 3: No secret has to stay bad.

Throughout the Bible, every good context of the word "secret" will have something to do with _____ _____.

Jesus invites us into a secret _____ with Him.

There is a difference between doing secret things _____ Jesus and doing secret things _____ Jesus.

Video sessions available for purchase at
www.lifeway.com/sacredsecrets

"Therefore I tell you, her sins, which are many, are forgiven—for she loved much. But he who is forgiven little, loves little" (Luke 7:47).

I have the first half of Luke 7:47 painted on the ceiling over my desk so I can point it out when the Enemy seeks to remind me of my past sins. How would you say the Scripture applies in your life?

In what ways do you need to point to the verse, whether or not you have it painted on your ceiling?

What other passage of Scripture might you need to point to when the Enemy harasses you? Write out the verses below.

As you read and study Scripture, listen to God for those passages He would want to burn especially deep into your soul or use to especially minister to you.

How do you react to this statement: People who have been deeply graced by God never withhold grace from other people, but people who don't feel like they've been terribly graced are the meanest people on the planet?

Explain why you agree or disagree with the statement.

Are you more prone to direct your meanness toward other people or to point it at yourself? Why do you suppose that's so?

"You have set our iniquities before you,
our secret sins in the light of
your presence" (Ps. 90:8).

Hebrew Word Study
`alam (צָלֵם): "to veil from sight," i.e. "conceal" (literally or figuratively); "to blind," "to hide or be hidden," "to hide oneself," "a secret thing," "to be concealed," or "to be secret"

Why do you suppose we persist in acting as if we can hide our secret sins from the God who knows every element of our lives down to the most minute detail?

Have you ever thought you had something hidden, behind a veil so to speak, only to have it brought to light? If so, how does having the veil of secrecy ripped away feel?

I believe that if we want anything guaranteed to manifest, we should go right ahead and keep it a secret.

Do you have a particular story or stories that illustrate the paradox?

Every defeat and every triumph of our lives comes from our vault.

"For you formed my inward parts;
you knitted me together in
my mother's womb.
I praise you, for I am fearfully
and wonderfully made.
Wonderful are your works;
my soul knows it very well.
My frame was not hidden from you,
when I was being made in secret,
intricately woven in the depths
of the earth" (Ps. 139:13-15).

How does the fact that God respected the process of creating you even when you were in your mother's womb impact you?

Do you feel like a wonderful work? Why or why not?

"I chose you before I formed you in the womb" could illustrate God's passionate desire to know you as soon as possible (Jer. 1:5, HCSB). He couldn't wait.

Throughout the Bible, every good context of the word *secret* will have something to do with God Himself.

Jesus invites us into a secret partnership with Him.

> "Be careful not to practice your righteousness in front of people, to be seen by them. Otherwise, you will have no reward from your Father in heaven. So whenever you give to the poor, don't sound a trumpet before you, as the hypocrites do in the synagogues and on the streets, to be applauded by people. I assure you: They've got their reward! But when you give to the poor, don't let your left hand know what your right hand is doing, so that your giving may be in secret. And your Father who sees in secret will reward you" (Matt. 6:1-4).

Secret in Matthew 6:4 is the word *kryptos* from which we get English words like *cryptic, encrypted, or cryptology*. Cryptology is code-breaking. To understand something that's encrypted, you have to dig. You have to work at it. That doesn't mean God's Word is in code. But it does mean that to understand God's Word you have to dig. He has riches reserved for those who will spend enough time with Him and in His Word to receive them. Here's the definition of *kryptos:*

Greek Word Study

kryptos (κρυπτός): "hidden," "concealed," "secret" (see Matt. 10:26; Mark 4:22; Luke 8:17; 12:2); "the inner part of man," "the soul" (see 1 Pet. 3:4); "in secret" (Matt. 6:4,6,18); "privately" (see John 7:4,10; 18:20); "he who is a Jew inwardly, in soul and not in circumcision alone" (see Rom. 2:29); "the hidden things of darkness," i.e. "things covered by darkness" (see 1 Cor. 4:5); "the things which men conceal" (see Rom. 2:16); "his secret thoughts, feelings, desires" (see 1 Cor. 14:25); "into a secret place" (see Luke 11:33).

Fun fact: The creator of the Superman comics story called the planet of his birth Krypton.

What have you gained from diligent study of God's Word that you might have missed without the effort?

Here's another paradoxical idea. Jesus said, "No one after lighting a lamp puts it in a cellar or under a basket, but on a stand, so that those who enter may see the light" (Luke 11:33). The word translated *cellar* is *kryptē* (κρύπτη). The message of Jesus is to be presented clearly, yet He reserves other truth for those who obey Him.

How might you decide what things ought to be set on the lampstand and what things ought to be kept *kryptos?*

How might the promise of Matthew 6:1-4 be fulfilled in the future kingdom of heaven?

If our present triumphs and defeats come from our secret place, how might the promise of Matthew 6:1-4 be fulfilled in the present manifestation of the kingdom of heaven?

Do you find it rewarding to follow after Jesus? If your answer is yes, think of the last time you felt a rush of it and describe it here as much as you're able.

One reason we don't feel more rewarded may be because we never go into the secret place where the reward would have come.

How do you respond to this idea?

How have you experienced the difference between doing secret things *for* Jesus and doing secret things *with* Jesus?

This element simply could not have greater emphasis in our journey. This part has been path-altering to me. At the risk of sounding completely cheesy, this paradigm shift has left me almost giddy in some of the secret partnerships Jesus and I are having now.

Do you see why doing something *with* Him could result in an even greater joy than doing something *for* Him? Explain your response.

The story of the attempted gift of the jacket reminds us that sometimes well-intentioned efforts to serve just don't work out. Just this morning my daughter Melissa and I went to that very coffee bar and, as we walked in the door, she looked at me and said, "Mom, promise me you're not going to try to take your shirt off and give it to her." We both laughed. I hope you grinned about the story too, but now that I've put myself out there, it's your turn.

Go ahead and share your own example of a time when your zeal was a little too much for someone and left you a bit red-faced. (Oh, I wish so much I could read your journal right now. Smiling.)

It's not always funny though. Sometimes we end up feeling like fools or failures even though God looks upon our well-meaning hearts and not our overzealous mishaps.

On this more serious note, how have you learned to cope when your attempts at ministry go awry?

How might you better cope in the future?

WEEK 4

YOUR FATHER
IN SECRET

> "But when you pray, go into your room and shut the door and pray to your Father who is in secret. And your Father who sees in secret will reward you" (Matt. 6:6).

I can't decide which idea in that familiar verse rocks my world the most.

The verse contains a tacit implication that first my Father in heaven wants me to come and meet with Him. How amazing is that, and how have we assigned such an earthshaking reality to the dry realm of the mundane?

Next, the fact that my Father has been waiting in secret hits me. I don't want to venture into performance and works here, so don't you do it either. But when I think of the times He doesn't seem near, could it be God wasn't distant? Instead was He waiting? Maybe I haven't experienced Him as much as I've wanted because He was in the secret and I was in the public?

Then I read about rewards. The best reward of all isn't the stuff God has for me. The greatest reward is Him. Oh, that I would fully dwell in Psalm 37:4:

> "Delight yourself in the LORD,
>   and he will give you the desires of your heart."

When I delight myself in the Lord, He rewards me with the delight of my soul: Himself.

I'm so glad you're along, dear one. Let's hasten to the secret place where our Father waits.

YOUR FATHER IN SECRET

Recap:
The Theology of Secrecy: Secrets Manifest

Our prayer: Lord, You teach me wisdom in the secret.

Point 1: There are bad secrets and there are good secrets.

Point 2: A bad secret can be the death of us.

Point 3: No secret has to stay bad.

Point 4: Our Father _____ good secrets.

Point 5: Our Father is _____ _____ in the secret.

Point 6: Jesus tells secrets of the _____.

Get in a _____ _____ and hide yourself.

There's one secret we never want to keep to ourselves: the _____ _____ of Jesus Christ.

Video sessions available for purchase at
www.lifeway.com/sacredsecrets

"So they took away the stone. And Jesus lifted up his eyes and said, 'Father, I thank you that you have heard me. I knew that you always hear me, but I said this on account of the people standing around, that they may believe that you sent me'" (John 11:41-42).

Which part of John 11:41-42 impacts you most?

Explain below your response to Jesus' actions in John 11.

that Jesus thanked the Father for hearing even before He heard

that Jesus knew that the Father always heard Him

that Jesus was concerned that the bystanders, including you and me, would believe

that Jesus raised Lazarus from the dead

Anything else do you want to add?

What might happen if you prayed like Jesus was
actually sitting with you now?

What interferes most with your having more of a
secret life with Jesus?

Meditate for a moment on the picture Isaiah paints of where our attempts to hide from God take us.

> "sitting among the graves,
> spending nights in secret places,
> eating the meat of pigs,
> and putting polluted broth in their
> bowls" (Isa. 65:4, HCSB).

Hebrew Word Study

"Secret places" in the verse is translated from *natsar* (נָצַר) meaning "to guard," in a good sense: "to protect, maintain, obey," or in a bad sense: "to conceal," "besieged," "hidden thing," "keep," "observe," "preserve," "subtil," or "watcher."

You've heard the statement that sin will
take you further than you want to go,
keep you longer than you want to stay, and
cost you more than you want to pay.

For thousands of years, God's primary efforts have been to save you from that destination. Take a moment to express your thoughts and feelings to Him about His plan.

Point 5: Our Father is with us in the secret.

> "Then the disciples came and said to him, 'Why do you speak to them in parables?' And he answered them, 'To you it has been given to know the secrets of the kingdom of heaven, but to them it has not been given'" (Matt. 13:10-11).

Earlier we considered these verses, but now we've had more time to develop the concept. What are some of the "secrets of the kingdom of heaven" (Matt. 13:11) you have come to discover in your most recent years?

In Matthew 13 we encounter the second Greek term for *secret*. It's a word you will recognize. It transliterates as *musterion* or *mystērion*. Read the definition:

Greek Word Study

Mystērion (μυστήριον) in classical Greek is a "hidden thing," "secret," or "mystery." It generally refers to mysteries or religious secrets confided only to the initiated and not to be communicated by them to ordinary mortals.

Point 6: Jesus tells secrets of the kingdom.

> "For to the one who has, more will be given, and he will have an abundance, but from the one who has not, even what he has will be taken away" (Matt. 13:12).

If we ignore God's invitation to explore the secrets of the kingdom, we may lose touch with the things He has shown us in the past. How frightening is that?

We pay so much attention to what we want manifested because we operate out in this external realm. We so thoroughly crave manifestations that we tend to pay more attention to what we can do outwardly and externally. Ironically, we're now learning that the only guarantee we have of manifestation is for that which we do in the secret. Our secrets with Him will always be manifest. This really is a paradigm shift for me. Am I late to the party and you've known *and lived it* all along? Share your thoughts.

How does this truth impact your thinking?

In Acts 17:6 those persecuting the believers said they had "turned the world upside down." I think we want that said about us, too. Don't you? So, if we want our gifting to come out, let's get in the secret place with Jesus.

How does this challenge turn our usual way of thinking upside down?

Write about a time you tried to do something externally but nothing came of it. Then write about a time when you went to the secret place and God showed the result openly.

"He said to them, 'Is a lamp brought in to be put under a basket, or under a bed, and not on a stand? For nothing is hidden except to be made manifest; nor is anything secret except to come to light'" (Mark 4:21-22).

How does the context of Mark 4:22 radically alter the common assumption that the verse is talking about God exposing our shame?

"But David said to Saul, 'Your servant used to keep sheep for his father. And when there came a lion, or a bear, and took a lamb from the flock, I went after him and struck him and delivered it out of his mouth. And if he arose against me, I caught him by his beard and struck him and killed him'" (1 Sam. 17:34-35).

Have you also fought some ferocious battles in the secret place? Some figurative lions and bears that most people wouldn't realize you'd battled? What do those battles mean to you now in the aftermath of the struggle?

"He who dwells in the secret place of the Most High
Shall abide under the shadow of the Almighty" (Ps. 91:1, NKJV).

WEEK 5

SECRET WHISPERS & ROOFTOP SHOUTS

How great a paradox have we uncovered in this study? If we want anything to manifest, then we need to bring it into the secret place. If we hide the dark things in our lives, they're going to come out. But if we bring them to our Father in secret, then He deals with them on our behalf. We can't guarantee that they will never in any way come out, but we can guarantee He will take the shame out of them for us.

That's dealing with the dark side of secrets, but what has been such a revelation to me in this study is the good side of secrets. Here we are running around wishing we could do something powerful. We wish we could be somebody. We want a platform so people will pay attention to us. All the while the answer lies in the secret place nobody can see.

God is waiting there to give us better than the best we could imagine. He's waiting to use us in ways beyond anything we could ever do in the natural world. He's waiting to supernaturally empower us. But Sister, home base for His supernatural work is the secret place.

Oh, I want to come out of this study changed forever. I covet the same for you. May God do a work in us when we are in the secret with Him that will resound around this world and echo into eternity. I want it for me, and I want it for you. Lord, let it be.

SECRET WHISPERS & ROOFTOP SHOUTS

Recap:

The Theology of Secrecy: Secrets Manifest

Our prayer: Lord, You teach me wisdom in the secret.

Point 1: There are bad secrets and there are good secrets.

Point 2: A bad secret can be the death of us.

Point 3: No secret has to stay bad.

Point 4: Our Father rewards good secrets.

Point 5: Our Father is with us in the secret.

Point 6: Jesus tells secrets of the kingdom.

When we keep a secret deep within us that is dark and dangerous, _____ _____ _____.

Don't worry about your _____ until you have spent time in the closet.

God confides as a friend to those who _____ Him.

The challenge: Are you going to go _____ _____ with Jesus?

Point 7: Our friendship with God is as _____ as the secrets between us.

Our time is short. Will you wimp out or _____ _____?

Greek Word Study

Lathra (λάθρα) is an adverb found in the following four places, meaning "secretly" in the sense of "quietly" or "discreetly."

"So her husband Joseph, being a righteous man, and not wanting to disgrace her publicly, decided to divorce her secretly" (Matt. 1:19, HCSB).

"Then Herod secretly summoned the wise men and asked them the exact time the star appeared" (Matt. 2:7, HCSB).

"Having said this, she went back and called her sister Mary, saying in private, 'The Teacher is here and is calling for you'" (John 11:28, HCSB).

"But Paul said to them, 'They beat us in public without a trial, although we are Roman citizens, and threw us in jail. And now are they going to smuggle us out secretly? Certainly not! On the contrary, let them come themselves and escort us out!'" (Acts 16:37, HCSB).

In what sense would you say God has been quietly or discreetly working in your life?

What events in your life have taken years before you were able to look back and say God was working quietly for your good?

Hebrew Word Study

Some Hebrew words related to *secrecy* are associated with the physical body and how we hold secrets close to us. Let these definitions intrigue you.

Jacob's deceitful father-in-law, Laban, said regarding Jacob's escape:

> "Why did you flee secretly and trick me,
> and did not tell me, so that I might have
> sent you away with mirth and songs, with
> tambourine and lyre?" (Gen. 31:27).

The word *secretly* is *chaba'* (חָבָא), meaning "to hide oneself," by contraction from *chabab* (חָבַב), meaning "to love properly" or a "cherisher," i.e. "bosom."

Proverbs uses a different word with a similar body reference:

> "The wicked accepts a bribe in secret to
> pervert the ways of justice" (Prov. 17:23).

Cheyq (הֵיק) means "to inclose" or "the bosom" (literally or figuratively) —"bosom," "bottom," "hollow," "lap," "midst," or "within."

Don't those passages paint a picture of how we sit rocking our secrets, sometimes holding them close as treasures and sometimes gripping them to endure the pain?

Word studies are fascinating I think. Don't you?

When we keep a secret deep within us that is dark and dangerous, it will manifest. We know where to expose it.

Write Hebrews 4:15-16 here:

You and I get to decide what's going to be the secret. We're going to come out before God with that which is dangerous, poisonous, toxic, and dark. We're going to come into the light. Our secret place is going to be maintained for what is light and what is glorious.

Why do the things God shows us need time to mature before we shout them from the rooftop?

What negatives result from prematurely seeking a rooftop?

With maturity we find it particularly important to let what Jesus says to us soak into our secret place before we begin to shout it from our platform. Think about and describe how taking time to grow is essential for the following areas.

What may it mean for our pride?

What may it mean for our message?

How might premature shouting lead to failure? To Satan using it to attack us mercilessly?

Has God been showing you how this principle may have impacted your life?

Yep. We've got to eat it before we Tweet it. Don't worry about your rooftop until you have spent time in the closet.

Let's not go roof seeking or roof surfing. Let's go closet seeking, and that's the way we'll eventually find ourselves on a roof.

Why might a concept like this be hard for a young believer, full of holy passion and anxious to make it to the roof?

"The friendship of the LORD is
for those who fear him,
and he makes known to them his
covenant" (Ps. 25:14).

Hebrew Word Study

The term translated *friendship* is *çowd* (סוֹד), from the root *yaçad* (יָסַד), meaning "a session," i.e. "company of persons (in close deliberation)"; by implication, "intimacy," "consultation," "a secret assembly," or "secret counsel."

> "We used to take sweet counsel together;
> within God's house we walked
> in the throng" (Ps. 55:14).

If you were writing a description of the three or four most important qualities you need in an intimate friend, what might they be?

Consider that list along with Psalm 25:14. Why might God reserve the greatest intimacy for those who exhibit the qualities you described?

Why might God reserving such intimacy be in your best interest, even if it proves more difficult?

How can casualness toward God be dangerous to intimacy with Him?

God confides as a friend to those who revere Him.

Point 7: Our friendship with God is as deep as the secrets between us.

You've got about 10 minutes, eternally speaking, on this planet to do the thing God has called you to do. Will we wimp out or are we going to step up?

The Prayer:

I want to hear, Lord. Speak to me. I want Your words to jump off the page. I don't just want to be looking for a platform. I want some presence. I want the prophetic, Lord. I want You to come, show me, make Your Word come alive off the page. Confide in me.

The Challenge:

Are you going to go somewhere new with Jesus? Somewhere secret that just the two of you share?

The Question:

Are you going to be someone Jesus can confide in? How so?

The Commission:

My Dear Sister,
God knows everything about you—

  all that has happened,

    all that has you bound,

      all that is broken in your heart,

        all the rejection,

          all the betrayal,

  and He's waiting to hear from you.

Bring words with you. Tell Him everything. Tell on everybody.
Your secrets are safe with Him.

Now He wants to know if His secrets are safe with you.

Let Him bring light into your darkness. Let Him plant something in secret that He can manifest in public.

Your Jesus is inviting you to a deeper secret life with Him.
That's where He sets you free. That's where He plants the seed.

Girlfriend, do not seek a platform; seek His presence.

In time He will show you your rooftop, and you will get to shout it out.

"Now to him who is able to keep you from stumbling and to present you blameless before the presence of his glory with great joy, to the only God, our Savior, through Jesus Christ our Lord, be glory, majesty, dominion, and authority, before all time and now and forever. Amen" (Jude 24-25).

My Beloved Sister,

This whole concept of deeply developing a secret life with Jesus has been one of the freshest things God has done in my soul in the last year. My imagination is stirred up with divine possibilities, and I am exhilarated over the adventure of it all. I feel like crying as I say thanks, not only to God, but also to you. Serving women like you has caused me to seek Christ for riches and revelation that I might have been less desperate to receive had I not felt the sober responsibility of a call to teach. I have asked God over and over to not let my life extend a day past my passion for Him and for His Word. I cannot speak for next year or even the next week but I can tell you this, my fellow sojourner. In a paraphrase of the prophet Samuel's words, thus far the Lord has helped me (see 1 Sam. 7:12). Thus far, pursuing Jesus Christ is still the most exhilarating adventure of my entire life. He alone stirs up a holy fire, and He alone can sustain it.

I do not take serving you lightly. Nothing about me was worthy of the privilege. I am a pauper to grace and as much today as yesterday. May Jesus take each of us deeper and deeper into a secret life with Him. Right there He will entrust us with riches that will manifest on a rooftop to the glory of His name through the good news on our lips. For every gospel word is a good word, Sister.

With much affection,

Beth

IDEAS FOR SMALL GROUPS

While you can complete this study as a personal effort, one of the best ways you can benefit is to get involved in a meaningful small group. Maybe you are already in a group but want to connect more deeply. Maybe you need to start a small group in your neighborhood, at your church, or with women you know. Either way, here are nine ways to cultivate a sacred and special group that will strengthen your relationship with Christ.

1. Be small. A large group of women can be fun, but it's not always best relationally. Don't be exclusive, but keep your small group small. This encourages everyone to have a voice in the discussion and fosters an atmosphere for true connection. You don't want someone to feel invisible in a big crowd. Plus, smaller groups feel safer. People will be more open than they would in front of lots of strangers. Consider agreeing on a reasonable number (give or take) so that your group doesn't get too big.

2. Be choosy. Discuss new study ideas as a group, and select things that resonate with the women collectively.

3. Be responsible. Don't let one or two people shoulder the responsibility for the entire group. Everyone can pitch in and should contribute. Have a sign-up sheet to rotate bringing snacks. Let women take turns leading the discussion. Encourage everyone to say the closing prayer once in a while.

4. Be consistent. Meet regularly at the same time and location. Ask women to commit to showing up. If a woman doesn't think she will be able to make it to most sessions, encourage her to wait until your next study begins. No one is taking roll and checking off a list, but having women consistently show up creates an environment of trust. Also be mindful to end on time. Everyone has had to make an effort to fit this study into their schedules. Close when you said you would

so women can get back to their pets, relieve the babysitter, get in bed early, or do whatever they have planned with that time.

5. Be vulnerable. No one wants to be a part of a group where they feel like they are the only one with problems (and, therefore, won't share them). Set aside time for everyone to tell their stories—the milestones that have brought them to where they are today. No one's life is perfect, and realizing that everyone in the room has had bumps along the road is so refreshing. And the more vulnerable you are, the more others will open up.

6. Be trustworthy. Women need to be fully confident that this group is a safe place and what they say will not be repeated or discussed outside of their presence. Accept people exactly where they are without judgment. When women do share openly, remember that they aren't asking to be fixed. Many times the best thing to do is just listen. Wait to be asked for advice. And if you are asked, speak the truth in love and be open to the fact that what works for you might not work for another.

7. Be prayerful. Pray with and for each other. Set aside time at the end of each meeting for everyone to share a personal prayer request. This is not a request for your coworker's grandmother's sick cat. This is an opportunity to share real things about yourself. If fitting this into the allotted time won't work, have everyone write down their requests and exchange with someone they can pray for throughout the week.

8. Be hungry. Jesus regularly ate with His disciples, and we should follow His lead! Plan a meal between studies just to be together. Talk about day-to-day life, what study you'd like to do next, little known facts about each other, or all of the above.

9. Be together. Once a year, plan a retreat with these women you've grown so close to. A weekend away from your busy lives will allow you to make memories and bond like the sisters in Christ you are.

Sacred Secrets
Group Leader Guide

The following suggestions can give you ideas for leading a *Sacred Secrets* group. Always take the suggestions as a place to start, but pray and complete your own study. The point of a group study is to support each other as you apply God's Word to your lives. Since every group is different, and since you have unique strengths and weaknesses, combine these suggestions with your creativity to find the best way to conduct a group. We have supplied you with more ideas and questions than your group can possibly use. Select those you believe will be helpful. Remember that often the Holy Spirit will lead the group to minister to each other in ways this guide could never anticipate. Exercise the freedom to follow the Spirit's leadership while keeping the group on task.

Promoting the Group Study

Promote the group through church bulletin announcements, posters, community announcements, social media, and personal invitation. You will want to enlist an adequate number of small group leaders to provide a discussion group for every group of no more than 12 women. The large group can view the video sessions together but will need to break into smaller groups to discuss. At *www.lifeway.com/sacredsecrets* you will find downloadable promotion helps.

A Six-Week Group Plan

Because *Sacred Secrets* came out of the Greensboro Living Proof Live event, it's a different format than you may have done with other studies. You may custom design the group experience to fit the needs of your group and church. The suggested plan here is for a six-session group experience. In this format the group will work as follows:

Session 1: Get acquainted, distribute books, and watch the video for session 1. During the week, members will use the questions and journal for week 1.

Session 2: Discuss the questions and journal from week 1. Then view video for session 2. During the week, members will use the questions and journal for week 2.

Session 3: Discuss the questions and journal from week 2. Then view the video for session 3. During the week, members will use the questions and journal for week 3.

Session 4: Discuss the questions and journal from week 3. Then view the video for session 4. During the week, members will use the questions and journal for week 4.

Session 5: Discuss the questions and journal from week 4. Then view the video for session 5. During the week, members will use the questions and journal for week 5.

Session 6: Discuss the questions and journal from week 5. Then conclude the group. Consider ending with a fellowship meal and plan future ministry with outreach to other women.

Each week before your group session:

View the video session and complete your viewer guide. Make notes of anything your group may need to further clarify. After the introductory week, complete the questions in the study guide for the next discussion and select those you believe your group will want to discuss. This means you will be completing week 1 questions and journal while previewing week 2 video, and so forth.

Consider drawing from the suggestions in each week's leader helps that follow. Pray about what goals the session most needs to meet, and plan your lesson to accomplish those goals. You may wish to make up your own group discussion sheet to give group members. Members will relax into the experience more if they know where they are going.

Remain open to the Spirit's leadership. Sometimes a group member will come with a concern or question that will result in a wonderful group experience that will bless the entire group. Other times you may need to avoid letting someone hijack the group into side issues. Experience and reliance on the Spirit will help you to know the difference. You will probably find that you will never get it right every time. If the group members are getting into the material, praying, and studying Scripture, your leadership will bear fruit.

Session 1
THE THEOLOGY OF SECRECY

1. Welcome the women to the group. You may want to plan activities to get acquainted as is appropriate for your group.

2. Stress the importance of trust in the group. Though this is not a support group, members must commit to confidentiality to establish trust. You may want to develop a group covenant together. Emphasize that in no case does any member have to share, nor should they share anything that would harm themselves or others. We will be learning that God does not expect us to expose ourselves without discretion.

3. Watch the first session video, complete the viewer guides, and then discuss.

4. Encourage the women to spend some time this week thinking and praying about the topic. The material in this study guide/journal will provide them some helps for exploring the concepts in the study.

5. Pray together and dismiss.

Session 2
THE THEOLOGY OF SECRECY/ AUTHENTIC INTIMACY

1. Welcome the group.

2. Ask what insights members have encountered in their study this week. Lead the discussion of week 1 questions. You may draw from the following suggested questions, or if the women volunteer insights, simply guide the sharing.

Suggested Discussion Starters/Questions

- What insights have you had this week about how secrets are both positive and negative? How can they be a wonderful shelter or a detestable thing?

- In what ways have you seen that secrets manifest no matter how hard we try to keep them hidden? How do they affect things like our health, relationships, parenting, and the ability to trust others or God?

- How has the Most High been a protection or shelter to you recently?

- Why do you suppose that we all have things in our vaults that can cause us great shame?

- Why do we need each other to help us discover the things in our vaults that we cannot see by ourselves or that we are incapable of appreciating alone?

- How can dealing with the contents of our vaults be a bit like cleaning clutter, draining an abscess, or discovering lost treasure?

- In what sense is the truth of God open knowledge? In what sense is it closed to outsiders?

- On what basis does Jesus reveal the secrets of the kingdom to some people and not to others?

- How would you explain to a younger woman or to your daughter how she could tell the difference between keeping confidence and protecting a lie?

- Could you describe a time when greater joy came because you had to seek what God had for you? How does that change your perspective regarding facing challenges?

3. Watch the second session video, complete the viewer guides, and then discuss.

4. Pray together and dismiss.

Session 3
AUTHENTIC INTIMACY/THE REWARDS OF THE SECRET PLACE

1. Welcome the group.

2. Ask what insights members have encountered in their study this week. Lead the discussion of week 2 questions. You may draw from the following suggested questions, or if the women volunteer insights, simply guide the sharing.

Suggested Discussion Starters/Questions

- In what sense can our secrets steal away our lives?

- How have you experienced Satan building a fortress in your secret places?

- What have you learned that can help you to mentor a younger believer to avoid false intimacy on the one hand and dangerous isolation on the other?

- Why do you think God's way is revelation rather than exhibition?

- Discuss the ladder of intimacy concept. What insights does it illustrate? What happens if we rush intimacy or attempt more than what the other person can handle?

- What does "we're not called to intimacy with our entire social network" mean to you?

- How does the space of contradictions between our interior life and our exterior life give extreme opportunity to the Devil?

- Why do you suppose Hosea 14:2 specifies that in repenting before God we are to take words with us? How does actual spoken repentance mean more than internal thoughts?

- How will you incorporate in your life the idea of authenticity with all, transparency with most, and intimacy with some? Do you think you need to work on being more transparent, less transparent, or some of both?

3. Watch the third session video, complete the viewer guides, and then discuss.

4. Pray together and dismiss.

Session 4
THE REWARDS OF THE SECRET PLACE/YOUR FATHER IN SECRET

1. Welcome the group.

2. Ask what insights members have encountered in their study this week. Lead the discussion of week 3 questions. You may draw from the following suggested questions, or if the women volunteer insights, simply guide the sharing.

Suggested Discussion Starters/Questions

- What passages of Scripture would you share with the group that you have used to point to when the Enemy harasses you?

- How do you react to the statement: People who have been deeply graced by God never withhold grace from other people, but people who don't feel like they've been terribly graced are the meanest people on the planet?

- Do you tend to turn your "meanness" to others, to beat up on yourself, or both? Why?

- Do you have a particular story that illustrates the paradox that if we want anything guaranteed to manifest, we should go right ahead and keep it a secret?

- How does the fact that God respected the process of creating you even when you were in your mother's womb impact you?

- Do you tend to feel that you are a wonderful work? Why or why not?

- If our present triumphs and defeats come from our secret place, how might the promise of Matthew 6:1-4 be fulfilled in the present manifestation of the kingdom of heaven as well as in the future kingdom?

- How have you experienced the difference between doing secret things *for* Jesus and doing secret things *with* Jesus?

- Like me with my jacket story, would you wish to share your own example of a time when your zeal was a little too much for someone and left you a bit red-faced?

- How might we learn to better cope with moments when our ministry attempts go awry?

3. Watch the fourth session video, complete the viewer guides, and then discuss.

4. Pray together and dismiss.

Session 5
YOUR FATHER IN SECRET/SECRET WHISPERS & ROOFTOP SHOUTS

1. Welcome the group.

2. Ask what insights members have encountered in their study this week. Lead the discussion of week 4 questions. You may draw from the following suggested questions, or if the women volunteer insights, simply guide the sharing.

Suggested Discussion Starters/Questions

- What would you say interferes most with your having more of a secret life with Jesus?

- What are some of the "secrets of the kingdom of heaven" (Matt. 13:11) you have come to discover in your most recent years?

- How frightening is it to you that if we ignore God's invitation to explore the secrets of the kingdom we may lose touch with the things He has showed us in the past?

- How does the idea that if we want our gifting to come out, we must get in the secret place with Jesus to turn our usual way of thinking upside down?

- Can you identify a time when you tried to do something externally but nothing came of it? How about a time when God showed the result openly when you went to the secret place?

- How does the context of Mark 4:22 radically alter the common assumption that the verse is talking about God exposing our shame? Answer: The context shows that Jesus was talking about demonstrating the good news of the kingdom, not judgment on sin.

- What do your own private battles with "a lion and a bear" mean to you now in the aftermath of the struggle?

3. Watch the final session video, complete the viewer guides, and then discuss.

4. Pray together and dismiss.

Preparation for the Final Session

Plan how you will end the group. Consider a fellowship meal, the launch of a ministry project, or enlistment in additional opportunities. Seek to make the conclusion of the group something special and memorable rather than just another class. Make preparations ahead of time for whatever conclusion you plan.

Session 6
SECRET WHISPERS & ROOFTOP SHOUTS

1. Welcome the group.

2. Ask what insights members have encountered in their study this week. Lead the discussion of week 5 questions. You may draw from the following suggested questions, or if the women volunteer insights, simply guide the sharing.

Suggested Discussion Starters/Questions

- In what ways would you say God has been quietly or discreetly working in your life?

- What events in your life have taken years before you were able to look back and say God was working quietly for your good?

- Why do you think the things God shows us often need time to mature before we shout them from the rooftop?

- What negatives have you seen result from prematurely seeking a rooftop?

- How would you explain to a younger believer the concept not to go roof seeking or roof surfing but to go closet seeking and then you're going to find your rooftop?

- If you were writing a description of the three or four most important qualities you need in an intimate friend, what might they be?

- Consider your list in the question above along with Psalm 25:14. Why might God reserve the greatest intimacy for those who exhibit the qualities you described?

3. In the absence of a video message for this last session, execute your plans for this final session. Consider using the bonus video segments from the kit for this session.

4. Pray together and dismiss.

NOTES

NOTES

SEE
BETH LIVE!

If you enjoyed this study, you'll love
LIVING PROOF LIVE!

GO TO
lifeway.com/LivingProof
to find the city near you

LET'S BE FRIENDS.

VISIT OUR BLOG AT lifeway.com/womenallaccess

LifeWay | Wom

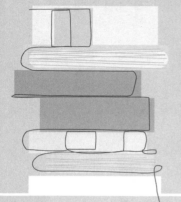

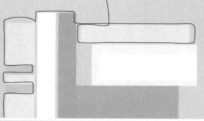
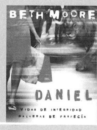

COMING IN
MAY
2014!

children
of the DAY

1 & 2
Thessalonians

BETH MOORE

LifeWay | **Women**